"*L is for Livermore* wonderfully illustrates, through insightful wor[ds,] one of the more underrated cities anywhere. There are countles[s reasons] Livermore feel so proud, and this fun yet information-packed boo[k...]"

DAN WOOD | Editor, *The Independent*

"*L is for Livermore* reminds us that learning doesn't just happen in classrooms... it's woven through our community. Every page celebrates the people, places, and pride that make Livermore such a vibrant place to grow and learn."

DR. DYRELL FOSTER | President, Las Positas College

"*L is for Livermore* is a wonderful tribute to the history and beauty of Livermore. Kori and Sammy have a done a beautiful job of capturing the best Livermore has to offer. I would recommend this book to anyone interested in learning more about our local treasures."

LIVERMORE VALLEY CHAMBER OF COMMERCE

"*L is for Livermore* captures the heart and spirit of the Western way of life. From barrel racers to parades, it's a joyful ride through Livermore's culture that kids and parents alike will love. This book belongs on every young cowboy and cowgirl's bookshelf!"

KATHLEEN MINSER | President, Livermore Rodeo Foundation

"A great way to explore Livermore for the family! This playful book will be your constant companion, helping you discover the stories and secrets behind lots of destinations around town. Tote it along as your checklist to Livermore adventures."

JEFF KASKEY | Historian, Livermore Heritage Guild

"A delightful blend of charm and local pride. With engaging rhymes and vibrant illustrations, this book celebrates the heart of the community while offering a meaningful glimpse into its history and spirit."

KARA KLOTCHMAN | Executive Director, Livermore Downtown Inc.

Visit us online | **WWW.HOMETOWNALPHABET.COM**

Instagram @HometownHighlightsAlphabet | **Facebook** Hometown Highlights Alphabet Series

Note From the Authors

It is simply not possible to squeeze a city's fullness into a few dozen pages and just as many paintings. The unique places, people, and compelling stories that make Livermore special are countless! So, here we are, merely scratching the surface with 26 highlights of the city's past (from the late 1800s) and present, in a way that kids and families can enjoy together. While many treasured destinations, history, and anecdotes could not be included, we hope that the sites and activities mentioned in the following pages kindle your desire to dig deeper into local history and inspire thankfulness for the beautiful place you call home.

The books in our Hometown Highlights Alphabet Series – *C is for Concord*, *W is for Walnut Creek*, *C is for Clayton*, *B is for Brentwood*, *M is for Martinez*, *L is for Livermore*, and those still to come – overflow from our hearts of thankfulness for the beautiful Bay Area communities where God has placed us. What began as a fun, simple local history project to give to our children grew into a gift of love for our community at large. We delight in words, books (they're good friends of ours), language, and art, and we strive to use our gifts to glorify God and bless our community through this series (1 Corinthians 10:31).

There are many terrific aspects that we love about writing and illustrating books, but we are particularly thankful for the connections with locals that we have made, and continue to make, on this journey. It makes us smile! And we hope that the paintings, poems, and history within these pages make *you* smile, too, and encourage you to learn more about your hometown.

Happy reading!

Kori & Sammy Barton

Husband-and-Wife Author/Illustrator Duo

To everyone at Gospel Community Church in Livermore,
without whom *L is for Livermore* would not exist.
♥ K.B. & S.B.
Soli Deo Gloria!

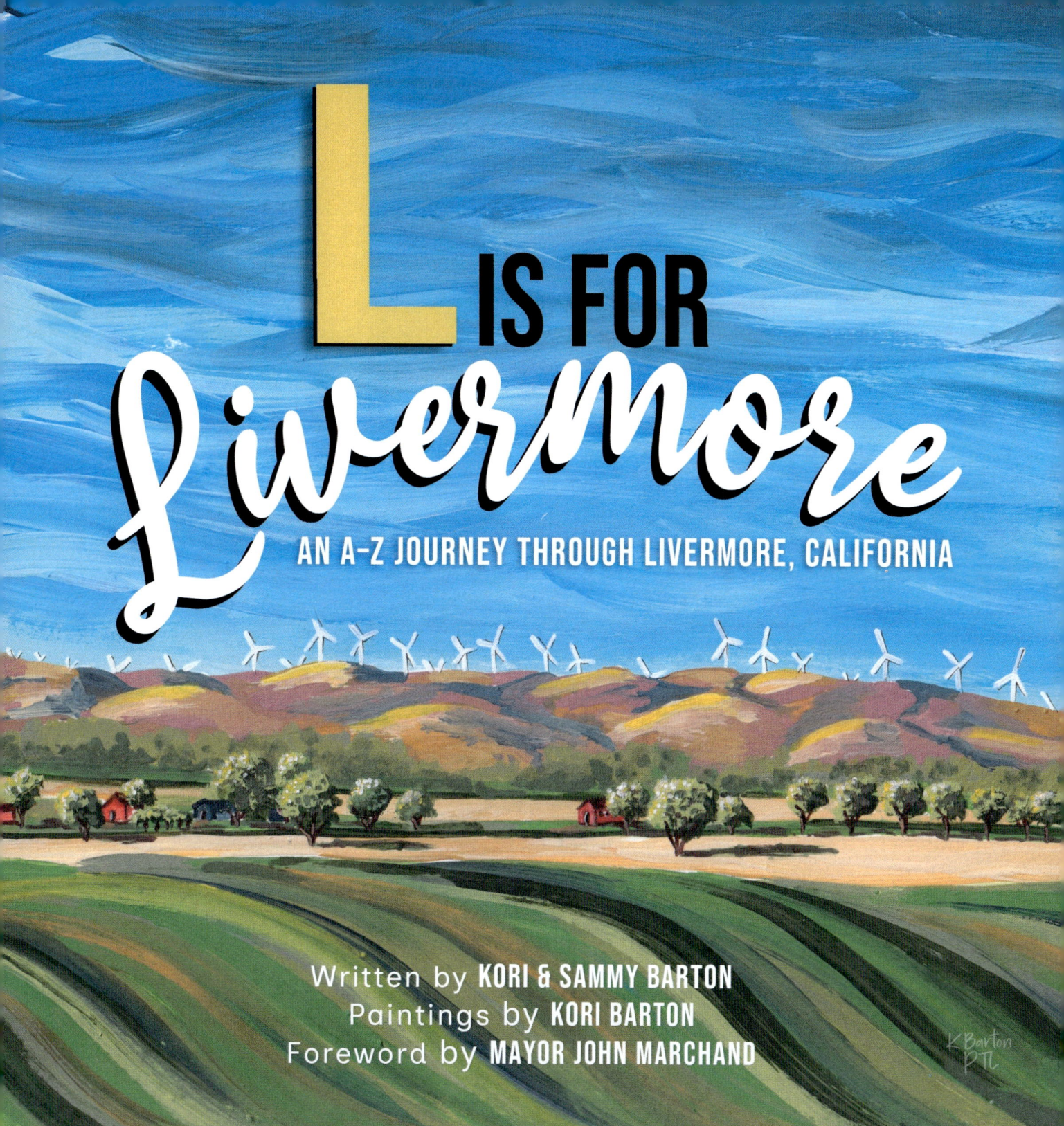

Foreword

L is for Livermore is more than an alphabet book—it is a love letter to Livermore. I hope it sparks pride in those who live here, and inspires young minds. This is a perfect gift for neighbors, friends, and future Livermore generations. It will become a keepsake for every Livermore family and classroom for years to come. It is a reminder that our past is rich, our present is vibrant, and our future is bright. Enjoy discovering, or rediscovering, the remarkable city we call home.

Livermore is a remarkable city of contrasts and superlatives. Livermore is California's oldest commercial wine region and, as the only city with two national laboratories, Lawrence Livermore and Sandia National Laboratories, we are at the cutting edge of technology. There is work that is being accomplished in Livermore that can be done nowhere else on Earth. Livermore has been called the "Smartest square mile on Earth." Livermore has the world's most powerful laser at the National Ignition Facility, which literally created a star on Earth.

The Transcontinental Railroad, which went through Livermore, was completed in 1869, the same year the town was founded. Coincidentally, it was also the same year that Dmitri Mendeleev created the Periodic Table of Elements. Livermore is one of only six cities in the world to have an element named after it and have our name appear on the Periodic Table of Elements; livermorium, element 116. I spent my career as a chemist, and now as Mayor, I am very proud of our city. I hope you enjoy this book about the city of Livermore as much as I do. Share it, gift it, and celebrate the place we love.

John Marchand

Mayor, City of Livermore
October 2025

Copyright © Kori Barton & Sammy Barton, 2025. All rights reserved.

ISBN 979-8-9895542-5-6

The illustrations for this book are rendered in acrylic paint, pencil, and ink.

No part of this book, including, but not limited to, text and illustrations, may be reproduced or used without prior written permission of the copyright owner. To request permissions contact the owner. Every effort has been made to contact copyright owners. The information in this book was correct at the time of publication, but the authors do not assume any liability, blame, or legal responsibility for reparation, monetary loss, damage caused by errors or omissions. The authors received no compensation from any of the individuals nor establishments nor entities included in this book. No statement in this book is intended to be a recommendation or a guarantee.

Contents

A IS FOR AIRPORT
B IS FOR BANKHEAD
C IS FOR CENTENNIAL LIGHT BULB
D IS FOR DEL VALLE REGIONAL PARK
E IS FOR ELEMENT
F IS FOR FOUNDER
G IS FOR GATHER
H IS FOR HAGEMANN RANCH
I IS FOR INTERSTATE
J IS FOR RANDY JOHNSON
K IS FOR KID-FRIENDLY
L IS FOR LIBRARY
M IS FOR MURALS
N IS FOR NUCLEAR
O IS FOR OPEN SPACE
P IS FOR PARADES
Q IS FOR QUAINT DOWNTOWN
R IS FOR RODEO
S IS FOR SYMPHONY
T IS FOR TURBINES
U IS FOR UNION HIGH SCHOOL
V IS FOR VINEYARDS
W IS FOR WORLD SERIES
X IS FOR TRAIN X-ING
Y IS FOR YEARLY FESTIVALS
Z IS FOR ZIP-AROUND

Honorable Mentions

How difficult it is to narrow Livermore down to 26 highlights!
Here are a few additional gems of Livermore's past and present:

LAS POSITAS COLLEGE (1963)
DONUT WHEEL (1962)
ALDEN LANE NURSERY (1955)
LIVERMORE TARWEED (ENDANGERED SPECIES)
VINE CINEMA (1956)
RAVENSWOOD HISTORIC SITE (1870S)
TREE SWEATER FOREST (2014)
DEACON DAVE'S CHRISTMAS LIGHTS (1982)

Aircraft soar through the city all night and all day,
at the Livermore AIRPORT, which starts with an A.
Each Fourth of July there's a huge celebration,
to remind everyone 'bout the birth of our nation.

The Livermore Municipal Airport (LVK) has been bustling with aircraft since it opened in 1965. However, in 1929 there was a private airport east of the current location. It was taken over by the Navy during WWII and called Livermore Sky Ranch. A few years after the war, the City of Livermore acquired the airport. Then, in 1963 it was sold to build a bigger and more modern airport: LVK. Much of today's airport can be seen from the public viewing platform on Terminal Circle. The airport covers more than 500 acres and houses 460 aircraft in hangars and outdoor tie-downs. In just one month, this busy airport handles approximately 16,000 operations (take-offs and landings). Each summer LVK hosts a massive Fourth of July event for the community, featuring dozens of historical and modern aircraft. If you look to the sky in Livermore on any given day, you're bound to see jets, bi-planes, helicopters, military aircraft, sky banner planes, and even blimps on occasion!

*B stands for BANKHEAD, with shows on the stage,
there are acts you'll enjoy there, no matter your age.
From concerts to plays and fun programs that teach,
it puts world-renowned entertainment within reach.*

The beautiful, 500-seat Bankhead Theater opened to the public in September 2007 and hosted more than 200 events in its very first season alone. Since then, the theater has seen its fair share of, "rock concerts, orchestras, world music, dance, comedy, magic, theater, stunt dogs and everything in between," says Chris Carter, current Chief Executive Officer of Livermore Valley Arts (LVA). More than one million visitors (and counting) have attended events at the Bankhead since 2007, and it now offers more than 250 events per year. Attendees can also enjoy the ever-changing art gallery displayed on the walls of the theater lobby that features wonderful local artists. "I love when I get to stand in the back of the theater during an amazing performance," says Chris, "and I can see how the show is impacting the audience." Chris wants you to know that, "the theater is for everyone," and the LVA team can't wait to show you to your seat at an upcoming production!

*The letter C stands for CENTENNIAL Light.
It's not much to look at; it's not very bright.
But since 1901 it's helped firemen get going,
and as far as we know,
it's the oldest bulb glowing!*

Who knew that a hand-blown incandescent light bulb given to the Livermore Volunteer Fire Department more than 120 years ago would become a world-famous gift that keeps on giving? In 1901, Dennis Bernal, owner of the Livermore Power and Light Company, wanted to help his hometown firefighting crew. His light bulb illuminated the fire department's hose-cart house to make gathering equipment easier and quicker in the dark. Since then, that same light bulb has continued to glow! It was moved a few times in Livermore over the decades, but it always turned back on. Why has it lasted so long? It is probably because the light bulb has only been turned off and on again a handful of times during its long life. Joe Testa, former Fire Chief of the Livermore-Pleasanton Fire District, says, "The Centennial Light draws visitors from all over the world to Fire Station 6." Just like the light is always on, the Livermore-Pleasanton Fire crews are always ready to help their community.

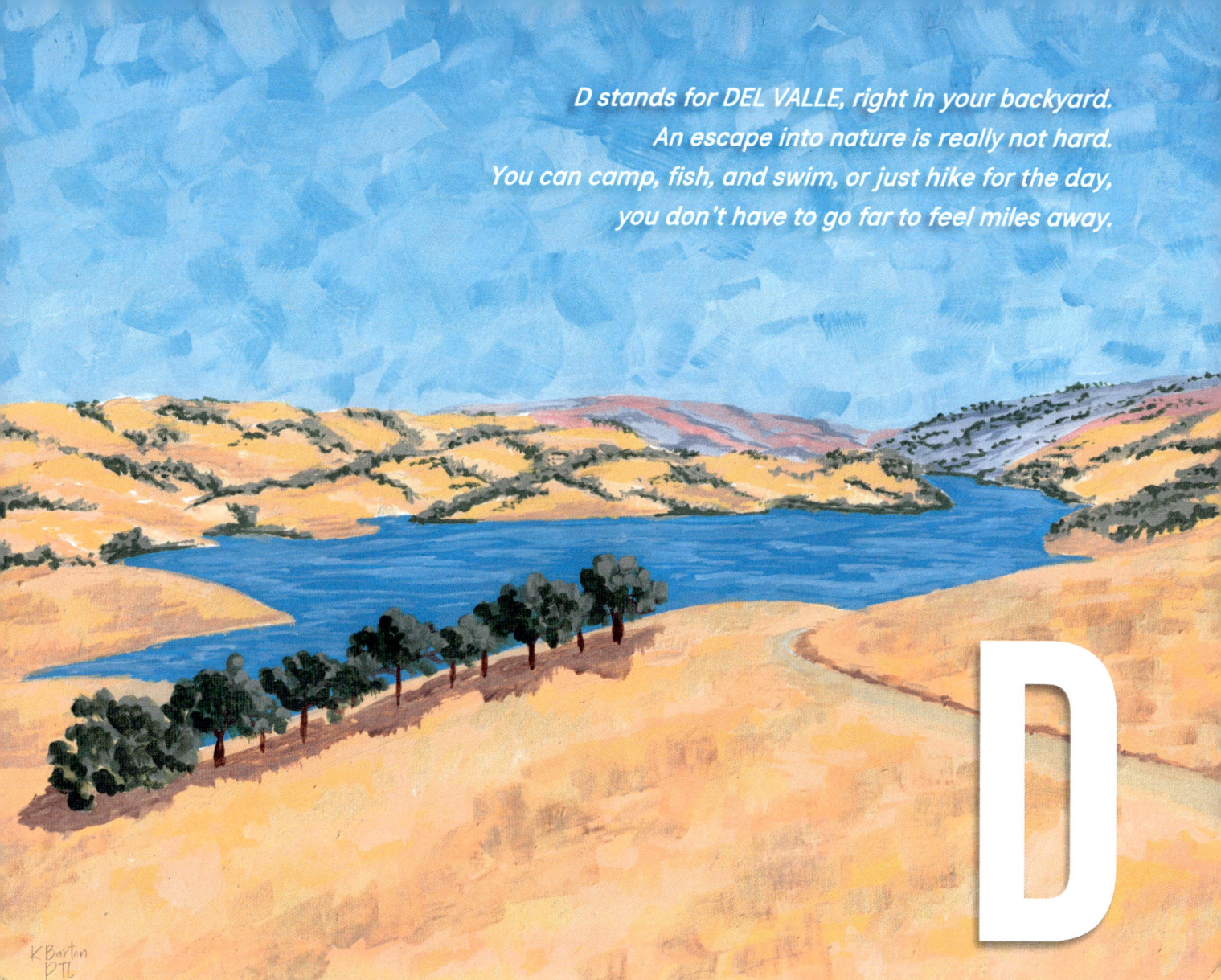

D stands for DEL VALLE, right in your backyard.
An escape into nature is really not hard.
You can camp, fish, and swim, or just hike for the day,
you don't have to go far to feel miles away.

The lush valley of Del Valle has been important for sustenance, work, and recreation for many people over the centuries. During rainy seasons, the Livermore area often flooded, so a dam was built in 1968 to prevent flooding and provide a supply of clean drinking water for the surrounding communities, thus creating a year-round lake. The East Bay Regional Park District (EBRPD) opened Del Valle Regional Park to the public in 1970 and welcomes about 400,000 visitors annually. The park is teeming with wildlife including pelicans, bats, tarantulas, and deer. The lake is stocked with trout in the cool months and catfish in summer. Ashley Grenier of EBRPD says that a special thing about this park is, "being near a large body of water and listening to the wind blow through the pines. It feels like you've escaped to the mountains, but it's right here in our backyard! It's a wilderness where you can choose your own adventure. Come for a lakeside picnic, stay overnight in the campground, enjoy the lake while on a boat, or take a walk or a hike."

E stands for ELEMENT, go look if you're able,
and find your town's name on the periodic table.
Elements are the stuff from which all things are made,
but you won't find ours out there, it all has decayed.

Only a few dozen places on Earth have elements on the periodic table named after them, and Livermore is one! So, what is livermorium? According to Lawrence Livermore National Lab (LLNL), "livermorium was discovered in 2000 by scientists at LLNL... It's a very rare and heavy element, and you can't see it or touch it because it doesn't last very long—it disappears really quickly!" And how did they make this element? "Scientists made livermorium by smashing other atoms together in a lab, kind of like putting puzzle pieces together to make something new. Even though livermorium isn't found in nature, learning about it helps scientists understand how the world works and discover new things." The Livermorium Plaza (pictured) was built in 2022 on South Livermore Avenue to commemorate this exciting discovery. You can visit the plaza to learn more and watch the mesmerizing livermorium atom water fountain spin around.

F stands for FOUNDER, and you probably thought, that his name must have been Livermore... but it's not! Mendenhall was his name, but he named the town for his friend and neighbor Robert L. Livermore.

A fellow named William M. Mendenhall (right) founded Livermore in 1869. The towering six-foot-tall pioneer traveled from Ohio by wagon with a dozen of his friends in 1845. He married Mary Allen in April 1847, acquired a vast plot of land in 1865, and then sold lots, thus beginning a new city. Why he didn't name the city Mendenhall, you ask? He named it to honor his friend and beloved local, Robert Livermore (left), who was born in London and settled in the Tri-Valley area as early as 1835. Robert is remembered as brave, generous, cheerful, and a friend to many. He thanked God for his nine children, his loving wife (California native, Josefa Higuera), food on the table, and a ranch to care for. His name, and the name of his land grant, Rancho Las Positas, is still sprinkled throughout the city, including the name of the community center, the golf course, the community college, street names, and more!

*A place folks would GATHER, which starts with a G,
was the library founded by ol' Carnegie.
It's now an art gallery and a museum
with cool things inside if you want to go see 'em.*

The first lending library in Livermore was established in 1875, with 250 books available for the community to borrow for a $3.00 annual membership. Three years later, a new library was established in a modest building that can still be seen today at 2136 First Street. Thanks to a grant from Mr. Andrew Carnegie's library foundation, the city built a larger library in 1911 called the Carnegie Library (pictured). For more than 50 years, this library acted as a center for learning and as a gathering place for the community. In those days, there were very few places where women and children could gather; this library provided the perfect, welcoming space for everyone. According to Jeff and Loretta Kaskey of the Livermore Heritage Guild, the basement of the library had a reading lounge for women and a special children's library. The Carnegie Library now serves as the Livermore Museum, a Livermore Art Association art gallery, and a hub for the Livermore Heritage Guild.

*H stands for HAGEMANN RANCH where you'll find,
tractors, barns, and farm critters of every kind.
The ranch was a bustling place in its prime,
but now you can go there to step back in time.*

A beautiful historic ranch sits on Olivina Avenue in west Livermore and gives a glimpse into what agricultural and ranching life was like in the 1800s. Martin Mendenhall, the brother of Livermore's founder William Mendenhall, purchased some 400 acres of land from Jose Joaquin Bernal's family, which was originally acquired by a Mexican land grant in 1835. The Mendenhalls lived on the ranch beginning in the 1860s and built a number of structures, many of which are still standing (pictured). The Hagemann family lived and worked on the ranch between 1896 and about 2006. The Livermore Heritage Guild now cares for the property, and it hosts open houses and events so the community can enjoy Livermore's past. When you visit, you'll see a blacksmith shop, the Mendenhalls' family home and garden, old barns, and friendly farm animals including horses, ducks, chickens, and goats.

I is for INTERSTATE, so autos could travel,
on concrete instead of on rough dirt or gravel.
The old Lincoln Highway can make the great boast,
that it was the first route to connect coast-to-coast.

The first interstate highway that stretched from New York City to San Francisco was called the Lincoln Highway, dedicated in 1913 to former President Abraham Lincoln. The road passed through Livermore, following modern day First Street and Portola Avenue. The Highway Garage (pictured) was built along the highway route in 1915 by local mechanic Frank H. Duarte. Travelers could easily stop for gas, tires, and auto repairs, which were oft needed back then as cars were far from reliable. Even when the highway was re-routed away from the garage, Frank (and later his sons) operated the business until the 1950s, mainly repairing farm and winery equipment. The garage still stands on the corner of Portola Avenue and North L Street, thanks to ongoing efforts from the Livermore Heritage Guild, which renovated it after protecting it from being bulldozed in the 1970s. It is home to many artifacts from the original business, as well as three restored fire trucks from the 20th century. Visitors are invited to the open houses that are held throughout the year.

J is for World Series champ, Randy JOHNSON,
a Hall of Fame pitcher whose career was awesome.
He pitched with a mix of endurance and power,
consistently one-hundred miles per hour!

Randy Johnson, National Baseball Hall of Famer, was born in Walnut Creek in 1963, and spent his childhood in Livermore, graduating from Livermore High in 1982. At seven years old, after his first day at Little League practice didn't go well and ended in tears, his dad helped him learn ball control by turning their garage door into a strike zone for pitching practice with tennis balls. The practice lessons with his dad paid off and he eventually became one of the most intimidating MLB pitchers of all time! This left-handed force earned many awards over his 22 seasons in the Majors, dominated in the 2001 World Series, and played his last season with the San Francisco Giants in 2009 winning his 300th career game. And remember the famous pitch that accidentally collided with a bird during the Arizona Diamondbacks' 2001 spring training? That was Randy, "The Big Unit," who now works with the Diamondbacks. Livermore honored Randy by naming the baseball fields at May Nissen Park after him in 2009.

If you want to bring smiles to your children's faces, you're in the right town, there's no shortage of places for families to visit and play for the day, Livermore is KID-FRIENDLY, which starts with a K.

K

In addition to miles of trails, parks, and open spaces in Livermore, there are fun, kid-friendly activities in every area of the city. At the Tri-Valley Quarter Midget Association, kids ages 5-17 have been racing their single-seater race cars around a track at 40 miles per hour since 1957, and dirt bikers have been getting down and dirty since 1995 at Club Moto Motocross Track. The Robert Livermore Aquatic Center (pictured) opened in 2005 and continues to be a popular summer spot for families. Granada Bowl has been a downtown feature since 1959 and welcomes 200-300 bowlers every week to their 32-lane center. Another favorite pastime for locals is miniature golf at Boomers (formerly Camelot Park, 1996) where folks play nearly 100,000 rounds of golf annually. In fact, mini golf has been a popular activity in Livermore for more than 100 years, with multiple courses throughout the city in the 1920s and 30s! There are dozens of other activities for kids and families in Livermore; far more than we have space to name.

L is for LIBRARY, a place to discover,
thousands of books, paperback and hardcover.
The topics are endless, learn brand new techniques;
take many books home and return in two weeks.

The Civic Center Library is a sight to behold, both inside and out. The library was constructed in 2004 joining a long lineage of library buildings in the city. Livermore esteems books and education so much that there are not one but three current Livermore libraries! Including the Springtown and Rincon branches, the libraries have more than 214,000 items in their collections combined, and in recent years, more than 947,000 items have been borrowed annually. "The library is the community's hub, and we get to be so many things for so many people," says Nathan Brumley with Livermore Library Services. Nathan and the library staff want locals to know that the libraries are a place where they can, "be inspired and discover the things that they want to learn about," or even just to have a quiet place to work on a puzzle. With year-round events for all ages, educational services, a Friends of the Livermore Library bookshop, and so much more, there is always something for everyone!

M is for MURALS, adorning your city.
Some tell a cool story and some are just pretty.
It's nice there's so many, because blank walls are boring,
look for artwork 'round town when you go out exploring.

The art culture in Livermore has been taken up a notch through large, colorful murals. Artists often work for two weeks or more to create a mural, and across the city you can find dozens of them in all shapes and sizes. Some are easy to find, like huge whales that were painted on the Water Reclamation Plant in 2010, and others are off the beaten path. Some murals tell a story, and others are simply a vibrant feast for the eyes. Many of the now-iconic murals downtown, including the "Welcome to Livermore" mural, began with an idea from local artist Trent Thompson. His idea turned into 14 colorful murals in 2020-2021 with a team of ten artists and an art grant from the City of Livermore. Trent felt that the city had, "a lot of big, blank walls that had potential. We had a cool opportunity to change that and create some momentum." "There are ongoing mural projects in Livermore that I didn't produce," he continues, "and that makes me feel like maybe I started something bigger than me, and all of it just because I had an idea."

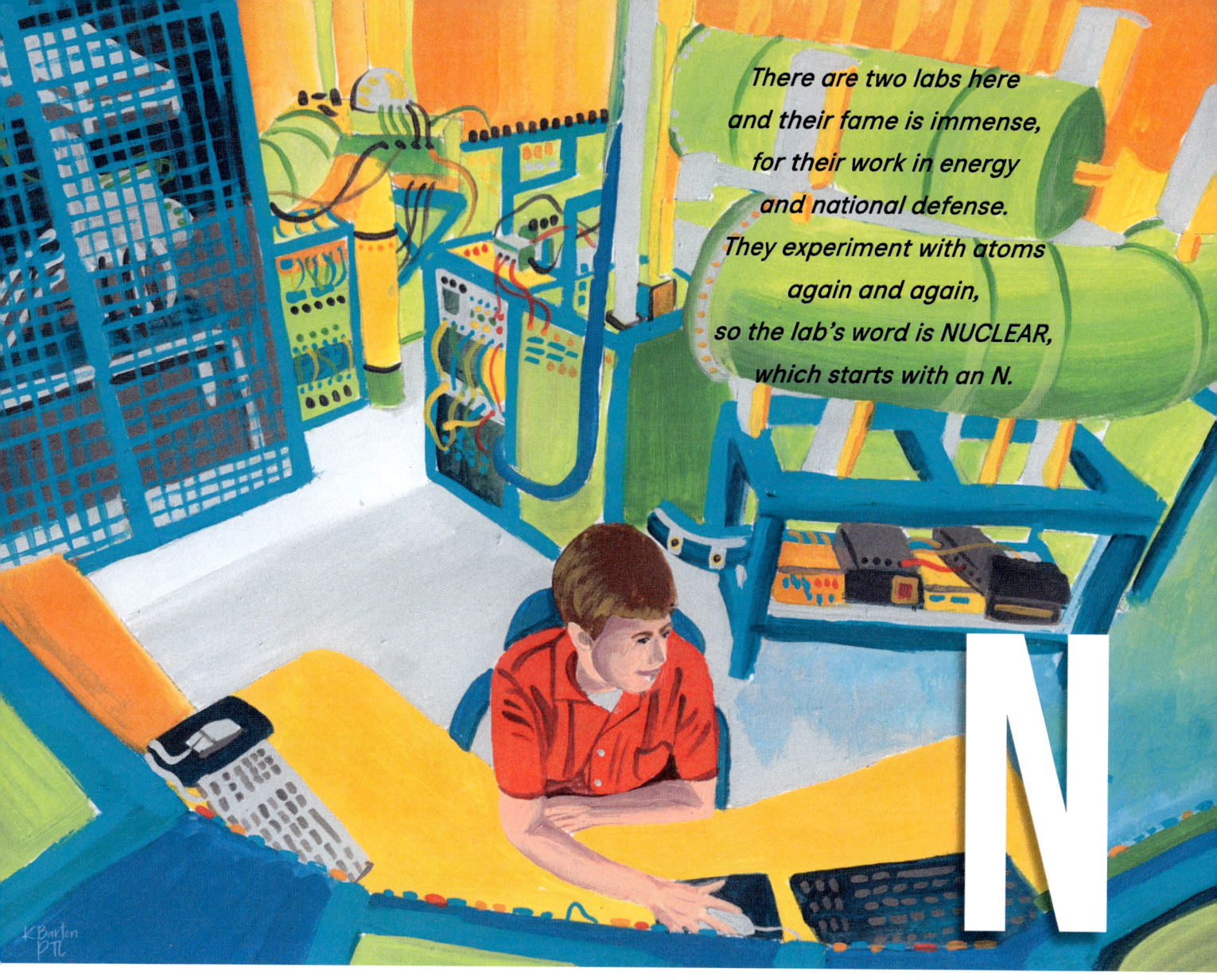

There are two labs here
and their fame is immense,
for their work in energy
and national defense.
They experiment with atoms
again and again,
so the lab's word is NUCLEAR,
which starts with an N.

Livermore is home to two important laboratories in the field of nuclear science: Lawrence Livermore National Lab (LLNL, established in 1952) and Sandia National Laboratories (established in 1956). According to LLNL, its team of scientists and engineers have worked together, "to solve tricky puzzles, discover new things, and invent technology. They study things like energy, space, and tiny atoms, all to help protect our country and make sure our future is bright and safe… our amazing scientists and engineers are like real-life superheroes!" About 9,000 people work at the lab and collaborate daily to, "use their brains and creativity to solve some of the world's coolest and trickiest problems. And we're also working hard to inspire future scientists—maybe even you!" Take a trip to the LLNL Discovery Center (est. 1976), an interactive "science playground" open to the public featuring hands-on exhibits that explain the exciting work going on at the lab every day.

If you're ever stuck wondering, "Where should I go?"
Try the four OPEN SPACES, which starts with an O.
Once grain fields, now wetlands. Once a dairy, now park.
You can wander the trails from dawn until dark.

O

Livermore is surrounded by open spaces and rolling hills just begging for adventure! The Livermore Area Recreation and Park District (LARPD) has 15 employees specifically dedicated to caring for four large open spaces in Livermore. The four open spaces collectively cover 1,430 acres and offer unique views, hikes, wildlife, and history. Holdener Park (pictured) was named after a beloved local family that owned a dairy as well as a dairy drive-through between 1931-1980. Brushy Peak (owned in cooperation with the East Bay Regional Parks District) and Garaventa Wetlands were formerly home to grain fields and grazing cattle during the late 19th-early 20th centuries. Sycamore Grove holds a secret: one of the oldest buildings in the area has been nestled in the park since 1885 when it was a winery and olive grove (Olivina Winery). Discover untold treasures when you hit the trails and spend the day exploring Livermore's open spaces.

*Several times every year
folks will march through the streets,
whether boy scouts or firemen or budding athletes.
Put your chair on the curb, find a spot in the shade,
be a part of the scene when P stands for PARADE!*

P

Annual parades have marched through downtown Livermore at least since the 1890s, and the number of faces in the crowd continues to grow. In recent years, about 15,000 people have turned out for the Rodeo Parade, a tradition that began in 1918. The Livermore Rotary Club has been organizing this parade since 1977, and it takes about 65 volunteers to make it happen. You just might see antique fire trucks, the Rodeo Queen, a stagecoach, mounted patrol, and marching bands. To celebrate the 100-year anniversary in 2018, cowboys even drove a herd of cattle right down the street! And while the Holiday Sights and Sounds Parade and Tree Lighting made its debut more recently in 1995, it instantly became a community favorite. It draws 28,000 locals, and it's no wonder! What other time do you get to see a gigantic grape harvester rolling through downtown decked out in sparkling lights?

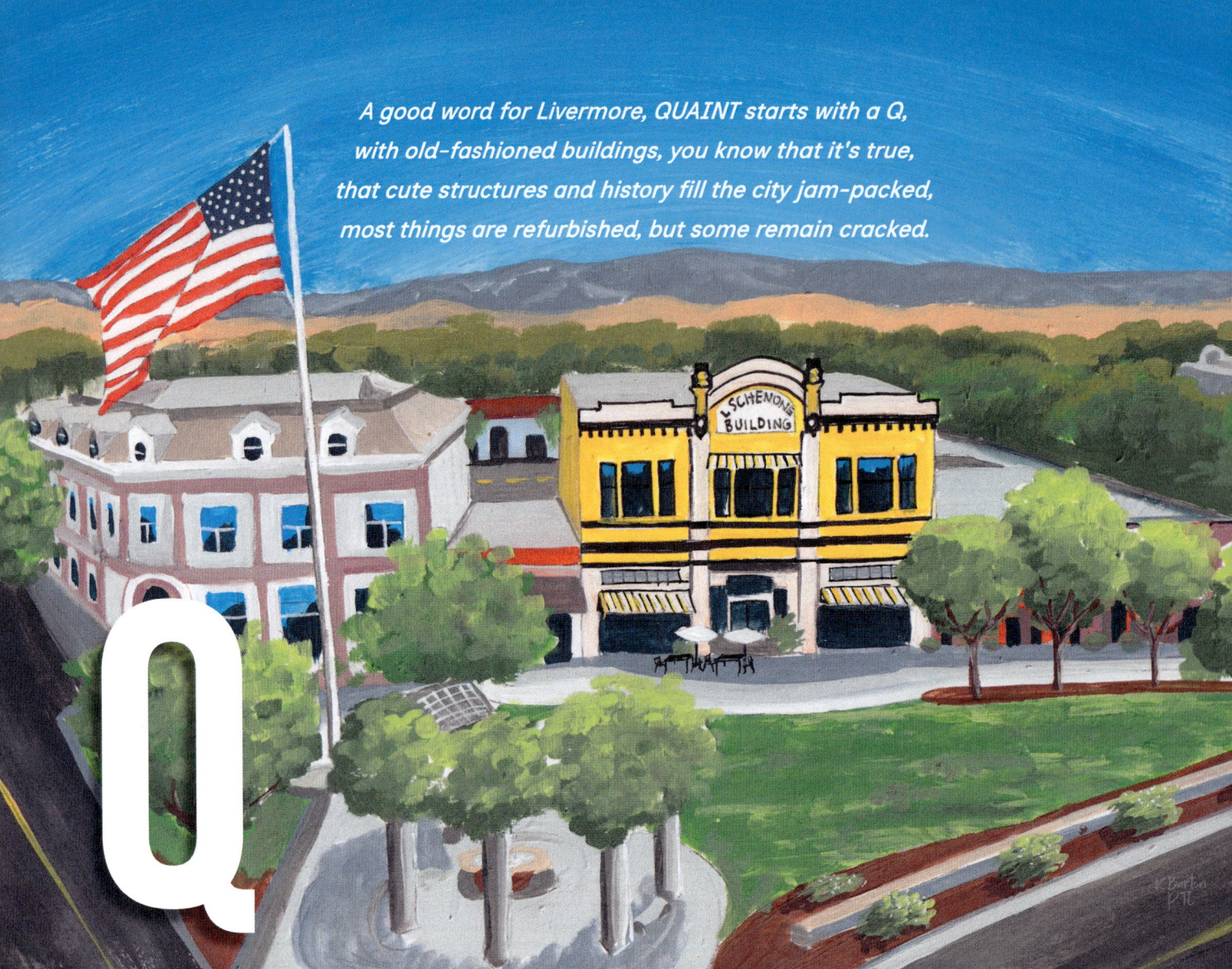

*A good word for Livermore, QUAINT starts with a Q,
with old-fashioned buildings, you know that it's true,
that cute structures and history fill the city jam-packed,
most things are refurbished, but some remain cracked.*

Downtown Livermore overflows with a remarkable history, plenty of charm, and it is the epitome of the word "quaint." Downtown has been a hub for the community since the late 1800s. Townsfolk would walk downtown to go to church, do banking, fetch mail at the post office, and buy supplies at Baughman's Western Outfitters, which is still operating over 140 years later! Though numerous original buildings were burned in fires or were removed to make way for new structures, many historical buildings remain, such as the Bank of Italy building from 1921, and the Schenone Building from 1914 (pictured). In 2009, Livermore was recognized with the Great American Main Street Award for its efforts to preserve and revitalize the historic downtown. As you walk through the streets, look for historic plaques that tell of the days when First Street was a simple, sunny dirt road. Livermore is a terrific place to call home and learn about the generations that came before.

The R is for RODEO. What else would it be?
Those cowboys and cowgirls are something to see.
They can gallop like lightning, then stop on a dime,
then rope 'em and tie 'em in world-record time.

The first annual Livermore Rodeo was held in 1918 to raise money for the Red Cross during WWI. Little did anyone know that the event would continue for more than a century! Today's famous "World's Fastest Rodeo" is supported by about 500 volunteers and draws about 16,000 attendees each year who watch more than 250 cowboys and cowgirls from all over the world compete. Many of them run family ranches, and the rodeo is a chance for them to show off the skills they use in their daily lives. The Livermore Rodeo Foundation (LRF) in 2008 began to support community and keep, "the spirit, heritage, and tradition of agriculture, ranching and rodeo alive." Current LRF President Kathleen Minser has been a part of the rodeo for nearly 30 years and always loves, "seeing the community at the event and keeping Western heritage alive!" In 2025, the Livermore Rodeo was inducted into the ProRodeo Hall of Fame; a huge honor for Livermore and its ranching roots.

S is for the Livermore-Amador SYMPHONY,
full of violins, piccolos, and even a timpani.
This group of professionals puts on a great show,
performing in *forte* and *pianissimo*.

The Livermore-Amador Symphony (LAS) was established in 1963 when locals wanted a way to use and express their musical talents. Since its first concert on January 25, 1964, this community-based symphony, comprised of local volunteers, has been delighting audiences of every age. "There is always a lot of action on the stage during a performance," says Lara Webber, conductor for the LAS since 2014. "The conductor dances around and shapes the music with their body, the string players make sound moving the bow across the string, and keep your eye on the cymbal player; they don't play for a long stretches, and then suddenly their golden circular cymbals crash together when the music reaches its most exciting point!" Lara wants locals to know that, "This is your orchestra! We are here for you!" The LAS visits schools to educate kids about the wonders of music and the symphony. Come see the symphony delight audiences at the Bankhead Theater throughout the year.

*Spinning 'round on the hills with their huge blades of three,
are the graceful wind TURBINES, which start with a T.
When you drive through the hills they're an iconic sight,
and they work to make energy both daytime and night.*

In years past, tower windmills harnessed the power of the valley winds as a practical way for early Livermore farmers to pump water for their homes and livestock. Wooden windmills were so popular that farmers could purchase them from local general stores. Fast forward one century and our windy valley got a big upgrade in 1981 with the Altamont Pass wind farm, one of the first large wind farms in the country. Colossal wind turbines stand about 430 feet tall, which is equivalent to 12 school busses lined up end to end! Perched on top of the tower are the 150-foot-long rotor blades. The turbine spins when the blades catch the wind, just like when you blow on a pinwheel. When the blades turn, it turns the generator (inside the box at the top of the tower), which creates electricity. The next time you drive past the wind farm, consider all of the lights, tea kettles, refrigerators, and lava lamps that turn on with a little help from our local wind turbines.

*Letter U stands for UNION HIGH SCHOOL, which is old,
since 1891 they have worn green and gold.
Think of all of the kids who have gone on succeeding,
'cause of teachers who taught them math, writing, and reading.*

Livermore High School was originally called Union High School in 1891. It was the first union high school in California, and it is one of the oldest remaining in the state. It shared space with a grammar school for two years before moving to the site where Bothwell Park now sits. The current high school building (pictured) was constructed on Maple Street in 1930 with 14 classrooms and a large auditorium. Much has changed at the school, including the name and many new buildings and sporting facilities, but it holds fast to its rich legacy and heritage. Current Principal Roxana Mohammed emphasizes that the school retains its sense of history by, "honoring traditions through events such as rallies, Homecoming, and our cowboy mascot and green-and-gold school colors." She continues, "a hallway in our main building displays historical class photographs and yearbook head shots. These photos begin as early as the 1920s and continue forward, providing a living timeline of our student body over the decades."

V is for VINEYARDS, with grapes on the vines,
they squish them and press them to make fancy wines.
Some people still stomp grapes into wine with their feet.
You might think that sounds gross, or you might think it's neat!

Robert Livermore planted the first known vineyard in Livermore in 1849, and a few decades later, C.H. Wente and James Concannon agreed that Livermore's climate would be ideal to create topnotch wines. Their two vineyards began in 1883 and are still producing award-winning wines as Concannon Vineyard and Wente Family Vineyards, the latter being the oldest continually operated family-owned winery in the country. Some of today's vines in these two vineyards were propagated from pieces of the "grandparent" vines originally planted more than 140 years ago! "Winegrowing is part of Livermore's big story," says Harrison Miller of Concannon Vineyard. "Some of the grapes here helped create what's now the most widely planted Cabernet in the country. So when you look at these vines, you're looking at a piece of American wine history that began in your hometown." Niki Wente is a fifth-generation winegrower who loves being a part of a family business and, "growing a product that can be shared and enjoyed. It's a very rewarding endeavor!" Vineyards are still an important part of the Livermore community with more than 40 wineries around the city.

*Each summer twelve teams from the world 'round descend,
upon Max Baer Park where they come to contend,
with bats and with cleats and with gloves on their hands,
in the Little League WORLD SERIES for which W stands.*

Little League entered the Livermore scene in 1956 and has had thousands of ballplayers through the decades, including Randy Johnson in the 1970s (see letter J). The Intermediate 50/70 Little League World Series has been hosted by Livermore's Granada Little League at Max Baer Park since the event's inception in 2013. Players in the Intermediate Division are 12 and 13 years old and teams come from all over the world to compete. The tournaments include teams from each region of the United States, as well as one team representing each of the following regions of the world: Asia-Pacific, Australia, Canada, Europe-Africa, Lain America, and Mexico. The annual Intermediate 50/70 Little League World Series draws thousands of spectators each year and is broadcast on ESPN.

X for railroad X-ING, the place where you stop,
for a train to go by when you see the arms drop.
It might take a while for a mile-long freight,
but that's fine, because you get to watch while you wait!

The first train rumbled through Livermore on September 6, 1869 and depots were constructed in 1870, marking the beginning of a thriving and bustling city. Trains carried hundreds of passengers and millions of pounds of freight each month, including coal, grain, wine, building materials, and animals. The railroad is owned by the Union Pacific Railroad (UP), and you can still watch mile-long UP freight trains chug down the tracks daily. The eye-catching purple ACE commuter train, run by the San Joaquin Regional Rail Commission, began in 1998 and stops at two stations in Livermore eight times each day. The ACE trains take about 850,000 passengers each year to ten stations between Stockton and San Jose. At the downtown Livermore station, you can still see the original train depot that was built in 1892 on L Street. It was carefully moved to the current location in the middle of the night on July 16, 2017 – an incredible feat of teamwork! It has been fully restored, including iconic colonial yellow paint with brown trim, and displays railway artifacts in the lobby.

*Y stands for YEARLY FESTIVALS in the town,
folks enjoy the biggest celebrations around.
See old cars by the hundreds and vendor-lined streets,
and come back the next time when each shindig repeats.*

Y

On any given weekend, there is some sort of festive event happening in the city. Livermore Downtown Inc. organizes several popular annual events including the year-round Farmers' Market (pictured), springtime Street Fest, Kidz Town Hay Day, and the ever popular Holiday Sights and Sounds Parade and Tree Lighting. Since 2001, Livermore Valley Arts has organized the ArtWalk showcasing about 200 local artists at vendor booths downtown. The Livermore Police Department hosts a Trunk-or-Treat event that packs the parking lot with decorated trunks and thousands of kids and their families. The City of Livermore hosts an incredible Fourth of July Celebration at the airport complete with vintage aircraft on display (pictured in letter "A"). The Altamont Cruisers club has managed the annual Nostalgia Day Car Show since 1990 and had 800 car entries in 2025. And, of course, we can't forget to mention the Rodeo (see letter "R"). Truly, this list is merely scratching the surface of all the happenings in the city!

*You can easily get from point A to point B,
on a bike or by foot or on horseback, feel free!
Even one famous bike race was Livermore-bound,
so it's simply no wonder Z stands for ZIP-AROUND*

Living in a valley basin has its perks, like being able to walk and bike all around town without a lot of hills to conquer along the way. In about 30 minutes, you can bike from one side of Livermore to the other. The city is crisscrossed with more than 70 miles of trails, not to mention still more miles of dedicated bike lanes, which have even been used in the Amgen Tour of California in past years. The winding trails are maintained by a hard-working crew of 28 folks from the Livermore Area Recreation and Park District (LARPD). They keep the trails safe and in tip-top shape for walkers, joggers, bikers, horseback riders, and more. Hit the trails every month of the year to enjoy different smells, sights, and sounds in each changing season. If you're feeling ambitious, the Arroyo Mocho trail system can take you all the way to Concord via the Iron Horse Trail. Alternatively, if biking around a dirt track is more your style, the BMX track on Patterson Pass Road has got you covered!

Location Information

Livermore Municipal Airport & Viewing Platform
636 Terminal Circle

Bankhead Theater
2400 First Street
Livermorearts.org

Centennial Light Bulb
Fire station 6.
4550 East Avenue
Centennialbulb.org

Del Valle Regional Park
7000 Del Valle Road
Ebparks.org/parks/del-valle

Livermorium Plaza: 116 South Livermore Avenue

Carnegie Library and Park: 2153 Third Street

Livermore Art Association Gallery:
Livermoreartsassociation.org

Livermore Heritage Guild: Lhg.org

Hagemann Ranch: 455 Olivina Avenue
Lhg.org

Duarte Garage/Lincoln Highway
926 N L Street
Lhg.org

Randy Johnson Junior Giant's Field
685 Rincon Avenue

Granada Bowl: 1620 Railroad Ave

Tri-Valley Quarter Midget Association
6978 Northfront Road

Club Moto Motocross: 7727 Altamont Pass Road

Boomers: 2400 Kitty Hawk Road

Livermore Public Libraries
Civic Center: 1188 S. Livermore Avenue
Springtown: 998 Bluebell Drive
Rincon: 725 Rincon Avenue
Library.livermoreca.gov

City of Livermore: Livermoreca.gov

Discovery Center at Lawrence Livermore National Laboratory
East Gate Drive/Greenville Road
Llnl.gov/community-education/discovery-center

LARPD Open Spaces
Holdener Park: 2995 Hansen Road
Brushy Peak: North end of Laughlin Road
Garaventa: Altamont Creek Trail, 6544 Altamont Creek Drive
Sycamore Grove Park: 1051 Wetmore Road
Aquatic Center: 4448 Loyola Way

Livermore Rodeo
3000 Robertson Park Road
Livermorerodeo.com

Livermore-Amador Symphony
Livermoreamadorsymphony.org

Altamont Wind Farm
Visible in the northeast of town, and from the 680 freeway

Union High School (Livermore High School)
600 Maple Street

Concannon Vineyards: 4590 Tesla Road

Wente Family Vineyards: 5050 Arroyo Road

Little League
Livermorelittleleague.com
Granadalittleleague.com

Train Station: 2500 Railroad Avenue

Livermore Downtown Inc.: Livermoredowntown.com

Livermore Train Depot/Museum
2500 Railroad Avenue

Schenone Building
Corner of S. Livermore Ave & First Street

Baughman's Western Outfitters: 2029 First Street

Alphabet Check List

CHECK-OFF EACH FAMILY-FRIENDLY ACTIVITY AS YOU COMPLETE IT, AND THEN ADD YOUR OWN!

- [ ] Find the oldest airplane at the airport during the Fourth of July festival
- [ ] Attend a show at the Bankhead Theater
- [ ] Find the Centennial Light Bulb through the bay doors at Fire Station 6
- [ ] Identify four species of birds at Del Valle Regional Park
- [ ] Read all of the facts listed on the atom water feature at Livermorium Plaza
- [ ] Find and read the historical marker about Robert Livermore in Portola Park
- [ ] Try out the vintage typewriter at the Carnegie Library Museum
- [ ] Attend an open house at Hagemann Ranch
- [ ] Visit the Duarte Highway Garage Museum during an open house
- [ ] Play catch at the Randy Johnson Junior Giants Field
- [ ] Borrow a book or two (or ten!) from the library
- [ ] Find at least 12 murals around town
- [ ] Learn something new at the Lawrence Livermore National Laboratory Discovery Center
- [ ] Find the hidden antique winery building in Sycamore Grove Park
- [ ] Attend each of the downtown parades
- [ ] Be a spectator at the Livermore Rodeo
- [ ] Keep an eye out for the crashing cymbals at a Livermore-Amador Symphony performance
- [ ] See wind turbines from the Brushy Peak trails
- [ ] Go for a walk on a trail near vineyards
- [ ] Count the cars of a passing Union Pacific freight train (can you top 180?)
- [ ] Bike across Livermore on the Arroyo Mocho Trail
- [ ] Check out the railway artifacts at the Livermore train depot
- [ ] _____
- [ ] _____

Share your adventures with us!
#HometownHighlightsAlphabet
@HometownHighlightsAlphabet

Acknowledgements

We extend oodles of thanks to all members of the Livermore Heritage Guild for your preservation of history and eagerness to share your knowledge with us, especially Barbara Soules, Alan Frank, Richard Finn, Jeff and Loretta Kaskey, and Harry Briley. Thank you for your time, encouragement, local knowledge, and willingness to assist.

Without you, Dan Wood and Cindy Hadden, this book would be riddled with typos and overused hyphens. Your eye for grammar, punctuation, and attention to detail makes all the difference. Thank you so much for the time and care you spent editing this book (along with your encouragement and care)!

We made numerous wonderful connections with the community and beyond throughout this project. For permissions, time, knowledge, and support, we are very grateful to each of you who helped shape this book. Thank you all! In no particular order: City of Livermore, City Manager's Office, Mayor John Marchand, Granada Bowl (Nick Rose), Livermore Area Recreation and Parks District (David Weisgerber, Michelle Newbould), Las Positas Community College (Dyrell Foster, Chip Woerner), The Independent (Dan Wood), Livermore High School (Roxana Mohammed), Livermore Public Library (Nathan Brumley), ACE/San Joaquin Regional Rail Commission Public Relations Office, Livermore Rodeo (Kathleen Minser, Alyssa Hoxie), Randy Johnson, Livermore Valley Arts (Chris Carter), Livermore-Pleasanton Fire Department (Joe Testa), East Bay Regional Park District (Ashley Grenier), Livermore Chamber of Commerce (Sherri Souza), Wente Family Vineyards (Nike Wente), Concannon Vineyards (Harrison Miller), Justin Probert, Livermore Amador Symphony (Tim Barry, Lara Webber, Anne Anaya), Phil Doyle Photography (Phil Doyle), Lawrence Livermore National Lab, Tri-Valley Quarter Midget Club (Kayla Buchanan), Boomers (Chris Beason), Livermore Downtown Inc. (Kara Klotchman), Livermore Little League (Nicole Von Glahn), eLivermore (Bill Nale), Livermore Rotary Club (Marc Roberts, Paul Szmyd), Love Livermore (Nicole Nicolay, Robyn Annicchero), ABG Art Group/Trent Thompson (OnlyUp crew: Madeleine Tonzi, Ari Takata-Vazquez, Lady Henze, Everyday Hooray, Ricky Watts, Timothy B., Jami Butler, Konorebi, Fasm), Baughman's Western Outfitters (Amanda Sanders), Union Pacific Public Affairs and Corporate Communications, and our helpful children.

About the Authors

The Hometown Highlights Alphabet book series is written and illustrated by the happy husband-and-wife team, Sammy and Kori; homegrown Bay Area natives and fellow avid bookworms who share a particular affinity for the English language. They love to use their gifts of words and art to give thanks to God (1 Corinthians 10:31). You'll find them with their kids biking on local trails, hiking in the open spaces, and playing ball at community parks.

If you would like to say "hi" or be notified about upcoming book releases in the Hometown Highlights Alphabet Series, please visit:

www.HometownAlphabet.com

References

Centennial Bulb (n.d.). Accessed from: https://www.centennialbulb.org/

Drummond, Gary (2004). Building a Library. Livermore Heritage Guild, Newsletter Vol. XXXIII No. 8.

Frank, Alan (2025). Frontier to City: Livermore, California

Homan, Anne Marshall (2007). Historic Livermore, California

Jensen, Phil (July 2025). Preparation Meets Opportunity. Accessed from: https://www.independentnews.com/news/livermore_news/preparation-meets-opportunity-at-intermediate-world-series/article_4831f297-9d56-4864-829a-454fab3f5691.html

Livermore Airport (n.d.). Accessed from: https://www.livermoreca.gov/departments/public-works/airport

Livermore Heritage Guild

Livermore High School (n.d.). Accessed from: https://livermorehigh.livermoreschools.org/our-school/about-us

Livermore High School Celebrates 125 Years (May 28, 2017). Accessed from: https://www.independentnews.com/livermore-high-school-celebrates-125-years/collection_fe73dc66-40df-11e7-b861-eb26d425df38.html

Livermore Municipal Airport and Vicinity Data (n.d.). Alamdea County Government. Accessed from: https://www.acgov.org/cda/planning/generalplans/documents/LVK_Ch4_Revised_120111.pdf&ved=2ahUKEwjq3Y3Jm4SOAxWOLUQIHWcfNcIQFnoECBoQAQ&usg=AOvVaw3uT9932i-XxZgTMTIrDadF

Livermore, California (n.d.). Accessed from: https://kids.kiddle.co/Livermore,_California

Mendoza, Jordan (March 22, 2022). Remember that time Randy Johnson's fastball killed a dove during a baseball game? Retrieved from: https://www.usatoday.com/story/sports/mlb/2022/03/24/randy-johnson-hit-bird-baseball/7154161001/

Nale, Bill (n.d.). Livermore History. Accessed from: https://www.elivermore.com/photos/Hist_lvr_downtown4.htm

Randy Johnson (n.d.). Retrieved from: https://sports.jrank.org/pages/2347/Johnson-Randy-Born-in-Walnut-Creek-California.html

Solving Wind Energy in Altamont Pass (n.d.): Accessed from: https://avaenergy.org/from-the-ceos-desk/solving-wind-energy-in-altamont-pass/

Strzemp, Jude (December 2024). Holiday Parade and Tree Lighting Draws Tens of Thousands to Livermore. Accessed from: https://www.pleasantonweekly.com/community/2024/12/10/holiday-parade-and-tree-lighting-draws-tens-of-thousands-to-livermore/

Strzemp, Jude (February 2025). Accessed from: https://www.pleasantonweekly.com/family-lifestyle/2025/02/03/then-and-now-presentation-revisits-del-valle-regional-park-history/

Winke, Jeff (2018). Capturing the Past. Accessed from: https://innovationtrivalley.org/itvlg-news/capturing-the-past-historic-livermore-winery-building-lives-on-in-a-3d-point-cloud

Made in the USA
Coppell, TX
23 December 2025